Scrumptious Cupcakes

Scrumptious
Cupcakes
for the perfect indulgence

First published in 2010
LOVE FOOD is an imprint of Parragon Books Ltd

Parragon
Queen Street House
4 Queen Street
Bath BA1 1HE, UK

ISBN: 978-1-4454-0439-4

Printed in China

Notes for the Reader
This book uses imperial, metric, and US cup measurements. Follow the same units of measurement throughout; do not mix imperial and metric. All spoon measurements are level: teaspoons are assumed to be 5 ml, and tablespoons are assumed to be 15 ml. Unless otherwise stated, milk is assumed to be whole, eggs and individual vegetables such as potatoes are medium, and pepper is freshly ground black pepper.

The times given are an approximate guide only. Preparation times differ according to the techniques used by different people and the cooking times may also vary from those given as a result of the type of oven used. Optional ingredients, variations, or serving suggestions have not been included in the calculations.

Recipes using raw or very lightly cooked eggs should be avoided by infants, the elderly, pregnant women, convalescents, and anyone with a chronic condition. Pregnant and breastfeeding women are advised to avoid eating peanuts and peanut products. People with nut allergies should be aware that some of the prepared ingredients used in the recipes in this book may contain nuts. Always check the packaging before use.

PICTURE ACKNOWLEDGMENTS
The publisher would like to thank the following for permission to reproduce copyright material
Front cover image: Cupcakes © Alexandra Grablewski/Getty Images

For front cover recipe, please see page 12

Contents

Introduction

Who can resist a cupcake? These diminutive cakes are loved by all and are the perfect little treat to indulge in at any time. They are easy to make, fun, pretty, and add that little touch of extravagance to any event, from a birthday to Christmas, and even weddings.

This book is full of tempting ideas to treat yourself, family, and friends and includes classic cupcakes through to more elaborate recipes to ensure you're never short of ideas for these irresistible and individual cakes.

Baking is a science as well as an art, so it is important to follow the recipes precisely. Before you start, read through the recipe and gather together all of the required ingredients and equipment. Special equipment is not necessary because most kitchens will have the essentials; these are kitchen measuring cups and spoons, mixing bowls, a wooden spoon, baking sheets, and muffin pans. Buying the correct liners is also important because they not only help retain that characteristic cupcake shape but also help keep them fresh and moist. Crimped paper or foil liners are perfect but you can also now buy reusable, silicone liners that are colorful and do the job just as well.

Follow the top tips on the opposite page to ensure perfect results and you'll soon realize there is no time like the present to dig out your apron, get baking, and rediscover the joy of baking a batch of cupcake delights!

• Turn on the oven before you start in order to preheat it to the correct temperature while you're mixing.

• Use the baking times for each recipe as a guideline only. Temperatures vary widely from appliance to appliance. Being aware of this will ensure the best results every time.

• Always use eggs at room temperature. If you store eggs in the refrigerator, remove them about 30 minutes before use to let them come up to room temperature.

• Avoid overmixing because this can create a heavy texture—beat the mixture until just smooth.

• Bake the cupcakes immediately once mixed because the leavening agents begin to act as soon as they're combined with liquid.

• Avoid opening the oven during cooking—this reduces the oven temperature and can cause cupcakes to sink. Do, however, check just a few minutes before the end of the baking time to see how the cupcakes are progressing.

• Test for doneness—the cupcakes should be well risen and springy to the touch.

Everyday Cupcakes

Lemon Butterfly Cakes

makes 12

generous ¾ cup self-rising flour

½ tsp baking powder

½ cup butter, softened

generous ½ cup superfine sugar

2 eggs

finely grated rind of ½ lemon

2 tbsp milk

confectioners' sugar, for dusting

frosting

6 tbsp butter, softened

1½ cups confectioners' sugar

1 tbsp lemon juice

Preheat the oven to 375°F/190°C. Line a 12-hole muffin pan with 12 paper liners or put 12 double-layer paper liners on a baking sheet.

Sift the flour and baking powder into a large bowl, add the butter, sugar, eggs, lemon rind, and milk, and beat together until smooth. Spoon the batter into the paper liners.

Bake in the preheated oven for 15–20 minutes, or until well risen and springy to the touch. Transfer to a wire rack to cool completely.

To make the frosting, place the butter in a bowl and beat until light and fluffy. Sift in the confectioners' sugar, add the lemon juice, and beat together until smooth and creamy. When the cupcakes are cold, cut the top off each cupcake, then cut the top in half.

Spread or pipe a little of the frosting over the cut surface of each cupcake, then gently press the 2 cut cake pieces into it at an angle to resemble butterfly wings.

Rose Petal Cupcakes

makes 12

½ cup butter, softened
½ cup superfine sugar
2 eggs, lightly beaten
1 tbsp milk
few drops of rose extract
¼ tsp vanilla extract
1¼ cups self-rising flour
silver dragées, to decorate

crystallized rose petals
12–24 rose petals
lightly beaten egg white, for brushing
superfine sugar, for sprinkling

frosting
6 tbsp butter, softened
1½ cups confectioners' sugar
pink or purple food coloring (optional)

To make the crystallized rose petals, gently rinse the petals and dry well with paper towels. Using a pastry brush, paint both sides of a rose petal with egg white, then coat well with superfine sugar. Place on a tray and repeat with the remaining petals. Cover the tray with foil and let stand overnight.

Preheat the oven to 400°F/200°C. Line a 12-hole muffin pan with 12 paper liners or put 12 double-layer paper liners on a baking sheet.

Place the butter and sugar in a large bowl and beat together until light and fluffy, then gradually beat in the eggs. Stir in the milk, rose extract, and vanilla extract, then fold in the flour. Spoon the batter into the paper liners.

Bake in the preheated oven for 12–15 minutes, or until well risen and springy to the touch. Transfer to a wire rack to cool completely.

To make the frosting, place the butter in a large bowl and beat together until light and fluffy. Sift in the confectioners' sugar and mix well together. Add a few drops of pink or purple food coloring to match the rose petals, if liked.

When the cupcakes are cold, spread the frosting on top of each cupcake. Top with 1–2 crystallized rose petals and sprinkle with silver dragées to decorate.

Banana Toffee Cupcakes

makes 4

5 tbsp butter, softened,
plus extra for greasing

½ cup light brown sugar

2 eggs, lightly beaten

¾ cup self-rising flour

1 small ripe banana, peeled
and mashed

topping

⅔ cup heavy cream

½ banana, peeled and sliced

2 tbsp dulce de leche
(toffee sauce)

1 tbsp grated chocolate

Preheat the oven to 375°F/190°C. Grease four 1-cup ovenproof dishes (such as ramekins) with butter.

Place the butter and sugar in a bowl and beat together until light and fluffy. Gradually beat in the eggs. Sift in the flour and, using a metal spoon, fold into the mixture with the mashed banana. Spoon the mixture into the dishes.

Put the dishes on a baking sheet and bake in the preheated oven for 20–25 minutes, or until well risen and springy to the touch. Transfer to a wire rack to cool completely.

For the topping, whisk the cream in a bowl until soft peaks form. Spoon the whipped cream on top of each cupcake, then arrange 3–4 banana slices on top. Drizzle over the dulce de leche and sprinkle over the grated chocolate. Store the cupcakes in the refrigerator until ready to serve.

Chewy Oatmeal Cupcakes

makes 8

3 tbsp soft margarine

3 tbsp raw brown sugar

1 tbsp dark corn syrup

⅔ cup rolled oats

4 tbsp butter, softened

¼ cup superfine sugar

1 large egg, lightly beaten

generous ⅓ cup self-rising flour

Preheat the oven to 375°F/190°C. Line a 12-hole muffin pan with 8 paper liners or put 8 double-layer paper liners on a baking sheet.

Place the margarine, raw brown sugar, and corn syrup in a small saucepan and heat gently until the margarine has melted. Stir in the oats. Set aside.

Put the butter and superfine sugar in a bowl and beat together until light and fluffy. Gradually beat in the egg. Sift in the flour and, using a metal spoon, fold gently into the mixture. Spoon the mixture into the paper liners. Gently spoon the oatmeal mixture over the top.

Bake the cupcakes in the preheated oven for 20 minutes, or until golden brown. Transfer to a wire rack to cool completely.

Iced Cupcakes

makes 16

½ cup butter, softened

½ cup superfine sugar

2 eggs, lightly beaten

generous ¾ cup self-rising
flour

sugar flowers, colored
sprinkles, candied cherries,
and/or chocolate sprinkles,
to decorate

icing

1¾ cups confectioners'
sugar

about 2 tbsp warm water

a few drops of food coloring
(optional)

Preheat the oven to 375°F/190°C. Line two 12-hole muffin pans with 16 paper liners or put 16 double-layer paper liners on a baking sheet.

Place the butter and sugar in a large bowl and beat together until light and fluffy, then gradually beat in the eggs. Sift in the flour and fold into the mixture. Spoon the batter into the paper liners.

Bake in the preheated oven for 15–20 minutes, or until well risen and springy to the touch. Transfer to a wire rack to cool completely.

To make the icing, sift the confectioners' sugar into a bowl and stir in just enough warm water to mix to a smooth paste that is thick enough to coat the back of a wooden spoon. Stir in a few drops of food coloring, if using, then spread the icing over the cupcakes and decorate, as liked.

Queen Cakes

makes 18

½ cup butter, softened,
or soft margarine

½ cup superfine sugar

2 large eggs, lightly beaten

4 tsp lemon juice

1¼ cups self-rising flour

¾ cup raisins

2–4 tbsp milk, if necessary

Preheat the oven to 375°F/190°C. Line two 12-hole muffin pans with 18 paper liners or put 18 double-layer paper liners on a baking sheet. Place the butter and sugar in a large bowl and beat together until light and fluffy. Gradually beat in the eggs, then beat in the lemon juice with 1 tablespoon of the flour. Fold in the remaining flour and the raisins. If necessary, add a little milk to create a soft dropping consistency. Spoon the batter into the paper liners.

Bake in the preheated oven for 15–20 minutes, or until well risen and springy to the touch. Transfer to a wire rack to cool completely.

Rocky Road Cupcakes

makes 12

2 tbsp unsweetened cocoa

2 tbsp hot water

½ cup butter, softened

½ cup superfine sugar

2 eggs, lightly beaten

generous ¾ cup self-rising flour

topping

¼ cup chopped mixed nuts

3½ oz/100 g milk chocolate, melted

2 cups miniature marshmallows

¼ cup candied cherries, chopped

Line a 12-hole muffin pan with 12 paper liners or put 12 double-layer paper liners on a baking sheet.

Blend the cocoa and hot water together and set aside. Put the butter and sugar in a bowl and beat together until light and fluffy. Gradually beat in the eggs, then beat in the blended cocoa. Sift in the flour and, using a metal spoon, fold gently into the batter. Spoon the mixture into the paper liners.

Bake the cupcakes in the preheated oven for 20 minutes, or until well risen and springy to the touch. Transfer to a wire rack to cool completely.

To make the topping, stir the nuts into the melted chocolate and spread a little of the mixture over the top of the cupcakes. Lightly stir the marshmallows and cherries into the remaining chocolate mixture and pile on top of the cupcakes. Let set.

Double Ginger Cupcakes

makes 12

1¼ cups all-purpose flour

1 tbsp baking powder

2 tsp ground ginger

¾ cup unsalted butter, softened

generous ¾ cup light brown sugar

3 eggs, beaten

2 pieces of preserved ginger, finely chopped

diced preserved ginger, to decorate

frosting

scant 1 cup ricotta cheese

¾ cup confectioners' sugar, sifted

finely grated rind of 1 tangerine

Line a 12-hole muffin pan with 12 paper liners or put 12 double-layer paper liners on a baking sheet.

Sift the flour, baking powder, and ground ginger into a large bowl. Add the butter, brown sugar, and eggs and beat well until smooth. Stir in the finely chopped preserved ginger.

Spoon the batter into the paper liners. Bake in the preheated oven for 15–20 minutes, until well risen and springy to the touch. Transfer to a wire rack to cool completely.

For the frosting, mix together the ricotta, confectioners' sugar, and tangerine rind until smooth. Spoon a little frosting onto each cupcake and spread over the surface to cover. Top the cupcakes with diced preserved ginger and serve.

Moist Walnut Cupcakes

makes 12

generous ¾ cup walnuts

4 tbsp butter, softened,
cut into small pieces

½ cup superfine sugar

grated rind of ½ lemon

½ cup self-rising flour

2 eggs

12 walnut halves, to decorate

frosting

4 tbsp butter, softened

¾ cup confectioners' sugar

grated rind of ½ lemon

1 tsp lemon juice

Preheat the oven to 375°F/190°C. Line a 12-hole muffin pan with 12 paper liners or put 12 double-layer paper liners on a baking sheet.

Place the walnuts in a food processor and pulse until finely ground. Be careful not to overgrind, or the nuts will turn to oil.

Add the butter, sugar, lemon rind, flour, and eggs and blend until the mixture is evenly combined. Spoon the batter into the paper liners.

Bake in the preheated oven for 20 minutes, or until well risen and springy to the touch. Transfer to a wire rack to cool completely.

To make the frosting, place the butter in a bowl and beat until light and fluffy. Sift in the confectioners' sugar, add the lemon rind and juice, and mix well together. When the cupcakes are cold, spread the frosting on top of each cupcake and top with a walnut half to decorate.

Frosted Peanut Butter Cupcakes

makes 16

4 tbsp butter, softened,
or soft margarine

generous 1 cup light brown
sugar

½ cup crunchy peanut butter

2 eggs, lightly beaten

1 tsp vanilla extract

1⅔ cups all-purpose flour

2 tsp baking powder

generous ⅓ cup milk

frosting

generous ¾ cup cream cheese

2 tbsp butter, softened

2 cups confectioners' sugar

Preheat the oven to 350°F/180°C. Line two 12-hole muffin pans with 16 paper liners or put 16 double-layer paper liners on a baking sheet.

Place the butter, sugar, and peanut butter in a bowl and beat together for 1–2 minutes, or until well mixed. Gradually beat in the eggs, then add the vanilla extract. Sift in the flour and baking powder, then fold them into the mixture, alternating with the milk. Spoon the batter into the paper liners.

Bake in the preheated oven for 25 minutes, or until well risen and springy to the touch. Transfer to a wire rack to cool completely.

To make the frosting, place the cream cheese and butter in a large bowl and beat together until smooth. Sift the confectioners' sugar into the mixture, beat together until well mixed, then spread the frosting on top of each cupcake.

Chocolate Box

Jumbo Chocolate Chip Cupcakes

makes 8

7 tbsp butter, softened

½ cup superfine sugar

2 large eggs

¾ cup self-rising flour

½ cup semisweet chocolate chips

Preheat the oven to 375°F/190°C. Line a 12-hole muffin pan with 8 paper liners or put 8 double-layer paper liners on a baking sheet.

Place the butter, sugar, eggs, and flour in a large bowl and beat together until just smooth. Fold in the chocolate chips. Spoon the batter into the paper liners.

Bake in the preheated oven for 20–25 minutes, or until well risen and springy to the touch. Transfer to a wire rack to cool completely.

Chocolate Cupcakes with Cream Cheese Frosting

makes 18

6 tbsp butter, softened, or soft margarine

½ cup superfine sugar

2 eggs, lightly beaten

2 tbsp milk

⅓ cup semisweet chocolate chips

1⅔ cups self-rising flour

¼ cup unsweetened cocoa

chocolate curls, to decorate

frosting

8 oz/225 g white chocolate, broken into pieces

⅔ cup low-fat cream cheese

Preheat the oven to 400°F/200°C. Line two 12-hole muffin pans with 18 paper liners or put 18 double-layer paper liners on a baking sheet.

Place the butter and sugar in a large bowl and beat together until light and fluffy, then gradually beat in the eggs. Add the milk, then fold in the chocolate chips. Sift in the flour and cocoa, then fold into the batter. Spoon the batter into the paper liners.

Bake in the preheated oven for 20 minutes, or until well risen and springy to the touch. Transfer to a wire rack to cool completely.

To make the frosting, place the white chocolate in a small heatproof bowl, set the bowl over a saucepan of gently simmering water, and heat until melted. Let cool slightly. Place the cream cheese in a separate bowl and beat until softened, then beat in the slightly cooled chocolate.

When the cupcakes are cold, spread a little of the frosting over the top of each cupcake, then let chill in the refrigerator for 1 hour before serving. Decorate with a few chocolate curls.

Mocha Cupcakes with Whipped Cream

makes 20

2 tbsp instant espresso
coffee powder

6 tbsp butter

½ cup superfine sugar

1 tbsp honey

generous ¾ cup water

1⅔ cups all-purpose flour

2 tbsp unsweetened cocoa

1 tsp baking soda

3 tbsp milk

1 large egg, lightly beaten

topping

1 cup whipping cream

unsweetened cocoa,
for dusting

Preheat the oven to 350°F/180°C. Line two 12-hole muffin pans with 20 paper liners or put 20 double-layer paper liners on a baking sheet.

Place the coffee powder, butter, sugar, honey, and water in a saucepan and heat gently, stirring, until the sugar has dissolved. Bring to a boil, then reduce the heat and let simmer for 5 minutes. Pour into a large heatproof bowl and let cool.

When the mixture has cooled, sift in the flour and cocoa. Place the baking soda and milk in a bowl and stir to dissolve, then add to the mixture with the egg and beat together until smooth. Spoon the batter into the paper liners.

Bake in the preheated oven for 15–20 minutes, or until well risen and springy to the touch. Transfer to a wire rack to cool completely.

For the topping, place the cream in a bowl and whip until it holds its shape. Spoon heaping teaspoonfuls of cream on top of each cupcake, then dust lightly with sifted cocoa.

Warm Molten-Centered Chocolate Cupcakes

makes 6

4 tbsp butter, softened,
or soft margarine

¼ cup superfine sugar

1 large egg

⅔ cup self-rising flour

1 tbsp unsweetened cocoa

2 oz/55 g semisweet
chocolate

confectioners' sugar,
for dusting

Preheat the oven to 375°F/190°C. Line a 12-hole muffin pan with 6 paper liners or put 6 double-layer paper liners on a baking sheet.

Place the butter, sugar, egg, flour, and cocoa in a large bowl and beat together until just smooth. Spoon half of the batter into the paper liners. Using a teaspoon, make an indentation in the center of each cake. Break the chocolate into 6 even squares and place a piece in each indentation, then spoon the remaining cake batter on top.

Bake in the preheated oven for 20 minutes, or until well risen and springy to the touch. Let the cupcakes stand in the pan for 2–3 minutes before serving warm, dusted with sifted confectioners' sugar.

Marbled Chocolate Cupcakes

makes 21

¾ cup soft margarine

1 cup superfine sugar

3 eggs

1¼ cups self-rising flour

2 tbsp milk

2 oz/55 g semisweet
chocolate, melted

Preheat the oven to 350°F/180°C. Line two 12-hole muffin pans with 21 paper liners or put 21 double-layer paper liners on a baking sheet.

Place the margarine, sugar, eggs, flour, and milk in a large bowl and beat together until just smooth.

Divide the batter among 2 bowls. Add the melted chocolate to one and stir until mixed. Using a teaspoon, and alternating the chocolate batter with the plain, put 4 half-teaspoons into each paper liner.

Bake in the preheated oven for 20 minutes, or until well risen and springy to the touch. Transfer to a wire rack to cool completely.

Double Chocolate Cupcakes

makes 18

3 oz/85 g white chocolate

1 tbsp milk

generous ¾ cup self-rising flour

½ tsp baking powder

½ cup butter, softened

generous ½ cup superfine sugar

2 eggs

1 tsp vanilla extract

topping

5 oz/140 g milk chocolate

18 white chocolate discs

Preheat the oven to 375°F/190°C. Put 18 paper liners in 2 muffin pans or put 18 double-layer paper liners on a baking sheet.

Break the white chocolate into a heatproof bowl and add the milk. Set the bowl over a saucepan of simmering water and heat until melted. Remove from the heat and stir gently until smooth.

Sift the flour and baking powder into a bowl. Add the butter, sugar, eggs, and vanilla extract and, using an electric handheld mixer, beat together until smooth. Fold in the melted white chocolate. Spoon the batter into the paper liners.

Bake in the preheated oven for 20 minutes, or until well risen and springy to touch. Transfer to a wire rack and let cool completely.

To make the topping, break the milk chocolate into a heatproof bowl and set the bowl over a saucepan of gently simmering water and heat until melted. Cool for 5 minutes, then spread over the top of the cupcakes. Decorate each cupcake with a chocolate disc.

Chocolate & Orange Cupcakes

makes 16

½ cup butter, softened

generous ½ cup superfine sugar

finely grated rind and juice of ½ orange

2 eggs, lightly beaten

generous ¾ cup self-rising flour

1 oz/25 g dark chocolate, grated

thin strips candied orange peel, to decorate

frosting

4 oz /115 g dark chocolate, broken into pieces

2 tbsp unsalted butter

1 tbsp dark corn syrup

Preheat the oven to 350°F/180°C. Line two 12-hole muffin pans with 16 paper liners or put 16 double-layer paper liners on a baking sheet.

Put the butter, sugar, and orange rind in a bowl and beat together until light and fluffy. Gradually beat in the eggs. Sift in the flour and, using a metal spoon, fold gently into the mixture with the orange juice and grated chocolate. Spoon the batter into the paper liners.

Bake in the preheated oven for 20 minutes, or until well risen and springy to the touch. Transfer to a wire rack and let cool.

To make the frosting, break the chocolate into a heatproof bowl and add the butter and syrup. Set the bowl over a saucepan of simmering water and heat until melted. Remove from the heat and stir until smooth. Cool completely until the frosting is thick enough to spread. Spread over the cupcakes and decorate each cupcake with a few strips of candied orange peel. Let set.

Chocolate Fruit & Nut Crispy Cakes

makes 18

10½ oz/300 g semisweet chocolate, broken into pieces

generous ⅔ cup butter, cut into cubes

¾ cup dark corn syrup

⅔ cup Brazil nuts, coarsely chopped

⅔ cup plumped dried raisins

7 cups cornflakes

18 candied cherries, to decorate

Line two 12-hole muffin pans with 18 paper liners or put 18 double-layer paper liners on a baking sheet.

Place the chocolate, butter, and dark corn syrup into a large saucepan and heat gently until the butter has melted and the ingredients are runny but not hot. Remove from the heat and stir until well mixed.

Add the chopped nuts and raisins to the pan and stir together until the fruit and nuts are covered in chocolate. Add the cornflakes and stir until combined.

Spoon the mixture into the paper liners and top each with a candied cherry. Let set in a cool place for 2–4 hours before serving.

Devil's Food Cake with Chocolate Frosting

makes 18

3½ tbsp butter, softened,
or soft margarine

generous ½ cup dark brown
sugar

2 large eggs

generous ¾ cup all-purpose
flour

½ tsp baking soda

¼ cup unsweetened cocoa

½ cup sour cream

frosting

4½ oz/125 g semisweet
chocolate, broken into pieces

2 tbsp superfine sugar

⅔ cup sour cream

**chocolate sticks
(optional)**

3½ oz/100 g semisweet
chocolate

Preheat the oven to 350°F/180°C. Line two 12-hole muffin pans with 18 paper liners or put 18 double-layer paper liners on a baking sheet.

Place the butter, sugar, eggs, flour, baking soda, and cocoa in a large bowl and beat together until just smooth. Fold in the sour cream. Spoon the batter into the paper liners.

Bake in the preheated oven for 20 minutes, or until well risen and springy to the touch. Transfer to a wire rack to cool completely.

To make the frosting, place the chocolate in a heatproof bowl, set the bowl over a saucepan of gently simmering water, and heat until melted. Let cool slightly, then whisk in the sugar and sour cream until combined. Spread the frosting over the tops of the cakes and chill in the refrigerator before serving.

Decorate with chocolate sticks made by shaving semisweet chocolate with a vegetable peeler, if liked.

Chocolate Butterfly Cakes

makes 12

1 oz/25 g semisweet chocolate, broken into pieces

generous ½ cup butter, softened

⅔ cup superfine sugar

generous 1 cup self-rising flour

2 large eggs

2 tbsp unsweetened cocoa

confectioners' sugar, for dusting

frosting

7 tbsp butter, softened

2 cups confectioners' sugar

grated rind of ½ lemon

1 tbsp lemon juice

Preheat the oven to 350°F/180°C. Line a 12-hole muffin pan with 12 paper liners or put 12 double-layer paper liners on a baking sheet.

Place the chocolate in a heatproof bowl, set the bowl over a saucepan of gently simmering water, and heat until melted, then let cool slightly.

Place the butter, sugar, flour, eggs, and cocoa in a large bowl and beat together until the mixture is just smooth. Beat in the melted chocolate. Spoon the batter into the paper liners.

Bake in the preheated oven for 15 minutes, or until well risen and springy to the touch. Transfer to a wire rack to cool completely.

To make the frosting, place the butter in a bowl and beat until light and fluffy, then gradually sift in the confectioners' sugar and beat to combine. Beat in the lemon rind, then gradually beat in the lemon juice. Cut the top off each cake, then cut the top in half. Pipe the frosting over the cut surface of each cake and push the 2 cut cupcake pieces into the frosting to form wings. Dust with sifted confectioners' sugar.

Feeling Fruity

Warm Strawberry Cupcakes
Baked in a Teacup

makes 6

½ cup butter, softened,
plus extra for greasing

¼ cup strawberry preserve

generous ½ cup superfine
sugar

2 eggs, lightly beaten

1 tsp vanilla extract

generous ¾ cup self-rising
flour

6 whole strawberries,
for decorating

confectioners' sugar,
for dusting

Preheat the oven to 350°F/180°C. Grease six ¾-cup capacity heavy, round teacups with butter. Spoon 2 teaspoons of the strawberry preserve into the bottom of each teacup.

Place the butter and sugar in a large bowl and beat together until light and fluffy. Gradually add the eggs, beating well after each addition, then add the vanilla extract. Sift in the flour and fold into the batter. Spoon the batter into the teacups.

Stand the cups in a roasting pan, then pour in enough hot water to come one-third up the sides of the cups. Bake in the preheated oven for 40 minutes, or until well risen and springy to the touch. If overbrowning, cover the cupcakes with a sheet of foil. Let the cupcakes cool for 2–3 minutes, then carefully lift the cups from the pan and place them on saucers.

Top each cupcake with a strawberry, then dust them with sifted confectioners' sugar. Serve warm.

Fresh Raspberry Cupcakes

makes 12

2¼ cups fresh raspberries
⅔ cup sunflower oil
2 eggs
¾ cup superfine sugar
½ tsp vanilla extract
2 cups all-purpose flour
¾ tsp baking soda

topping
⅔ cup heavy cream
12 fresh raspberries
small mint leaves,
to decorate

Preheat the oven to 350°F/180°C. Line a 12-hole muffin pan with 12 paper liners or put 12 double-layer paper liners on a baking sheet.

Place the raspberries in a large bowl and crush lightly with a fork.

Place the oil, eggs, sugar, and vanilla extract in a large bowl and beat together until well combined. Sift in the flour and baking soda and fold into the batter, then fold in the crushed raspberries. Spoon the batter into the paper liners.

Bake in the preheated oven for 30 minutes, or until golden brown and springy to the touch. Let the cupcakes cool in the pan for 10 minutes, then transfer to a wire rack to cool completely.

When ready to decorate, place the cream in a bowl and whip until soft peaks form. Spread the cream on top of the cupcakes, using a knife to smooth the cream. Top each cupcake with a raspberry and decorate with mint leaves.

Apple Streusel Cupcakes

makes 14

½ tsp baking soda

10 oz/280 g jar applesauce

4 tbsp butter, softened, or soft margarine

½ cup raw brown sugar

1 large egg, lightly beaten

1¼ cups self-rising flour

½ tsp ground cinnamon

½ tsp freshly ground nutmeg

topping

⅓ cup all-purpose flour

¼ cup raw brown sugar

¼ tsp ground cinnamon

¼ tsp freshly grated nutmeg

3 tbsp butter, cut into small pieces

Preheat the oven to 350°F/180°C. Line two 12-hole muffin pans with 14 paper liners or put 14 double-layer paper liners on a baking sheet.

First, make the topping. Place the flour, sugar, cinnamon, and nutmeg in a large bowl. Add the butter and rub it in with your fingertips until the mixture resembles fine breadcrumbs. Set aside.

To make the cupcakes, add the baking soda to the jar of applesauce and stir until dissolved. Place the butter and sugar in a large bowl and beat together until light and fluffy, then gradually beat in the egg. Sift in the flour, cinnamon, and nutmeg and fold into the batter, alternating with the apple sauce. Spoon the batter into the paper liners. Scatter the reserved topping over each cupcake to cover the tops and press down gently.

Bake in the preheated oven for 20 minutes, or until well risen and golden brown. Let the cakes stand for 2–3 minutes in the pans before serving warm, or transfer to a wire rack to cool completely.

Lemon Meringue Cupcakes

makes 4

6 tbsp butter, softened, plus extra for greasing

scant ½ cup superfine sugar

finely grated rind and juice of ½ lemon

1 large egg, lightly beaten

scant ⅔ cup self-rising flour

2 tbsp lemon curd

meringue

2 egg whites

generous ½ cup superfine sugar

Preheat the oven to 375°F/190°C. Grease four 1-cup ovenproof bowls (such as ramekins) with butter.

Put the butter, sugar, and lemon rind into a mixing bowl and beat together until light and fluffy. Gradually beat in the egg. Sift in the flour and, using a metal spoon, fold into the mixture with the lemon juice. Spoon the batter into the bowls.

Put the bowls on a baking sheet and bake in the preheated oven for 15 minutes, or until well risen and springy to the touch.

While the cupcakes are baking, make the meringue. Put the egg whites in a clean, grease-free bowl and, using a handheld electric mixer, mix until stiff. Gradually beat in the superfine sugar to form a stiff and glossy meringue.

When the cupcakes are ready, remove from the oven and spread the lemon curd over the hot cupcakes, then swirl over the meringue. Return the cupcakes to the oven for 4–5 minutes, until the meringue is golden. Serve immediately.

Spiced Plum Cupcakes

makes 4

4 tbsp butter, softened, plus extra for greasing

generous ¼ cup superfine sugar

1 large egg, lightly beaten

generous ⅓ cup whole wheat flour

½ tsp baking powder

1 tsp ground allspice

¼ cup coarsely ground, blanched hazelnuts

2 small plums, halved, pitted, and sliced

Preheat the oven to 350°F/180°C. Grease four ⅔-cup ovenproof bowls (such as ramekins) with butter.

Put the butter and sugar in a bowl and beat together until light and fluffy. Gradually beat in the egg. Sift in the flour, baking powder, and allspice (adding any bran left in the sifter into the bowl) and, using a metal spoon, fold into the mixture with the ground hazelnuts. Spoon the batter into the bowls. Arrange the sliced plums on top of the batter.

Put the bowls on a baking sheet and bake in the preheated oven for 25 minutes, or until well risen and springy to the touch. Serve warm or cold.

Tropical Pineapple Cupcakes

serves 12

2 slices canned pineapple in natural juice

6 tbsp butter, softened, or soft margarine

½ cup superfine sugar

1 large egg, lightly beaten

⅔ cup self-rising flour

frosting

2 tbsp butter, softened

½ cup cream cheese

grated rind of 1 lemon or lime

generous ¾ cup confectioners' sugar

1 tsp lemon juice or lime juice

Preheat the oven to 350°F/180°C. Line a 12-hole muffin pan with 12 paper liners or put 12 double-layer paper liners on a baking sheet.

Drain the pineapple, reserving the juice. Finely chop the pineapple slices. Place the butter and sugar in a large bowl and beat together until light and fluffy, then gradually beat in the egg. Add the flour and fold into the mixture. Fold in the chopped pineapple and 1 tablespoon of the reserved pineapple juice. Spoon the batter into the paper liners.

Bake in the preheated oven for 20 minutes, or until well risen and springy to the touch. Transfer to a wire rack to cool completely.

To make the frosting, place the butter and cream cheese in a large bowl and beat together until smooth, then add the lemon or lime rind.

Sift the confectioners' sugar into the mixture and beat together until well mixed. Gradually beat in the lemon or lime juice, adding enough to form a spreading consistency.

When the cupcakes are cold, spread the frosting on top of each cupcake, or fill a pastry bag fitted with a large star tip and pipe the frosting on top.

Coconut Cherry Cupcakes

makes 12

½ cup butter, softened,
or soft margarine

½ cup superfine sugar

2 tbsp milk

2 eggs, lightly beaten

⅔ cup self-rising flour

½ tsp baking powder

¾ cup dry unsweetened
coconut

4 oz/115 g candied cherries,
quartered

12 whole candied,
maraschino, or fresh
cherries, to decorate

frosting
4 tbsp butter, softened

1 cup confectioners' sugar

1 tbsp milk

Preheat the oven to 350°F/180°C. Line a 12-hole muffin pan with 12 paper liners or put 12 double-layer paper liners on a baking sheet.

Place the butter and sugar in a large bowl and beat together until light and fluffy. Stir in the milk and then gradually beat in the eggs. Sift in the flour and baking powder and fold them in with the coconut. Gently fold in most of the quartered cherries.

Spoon the batter into the paper liners. Scatter the remaining quartered cherries evenly on top.

Bake in the preheated oven for 20–25 minutes, or until well risen and springy to the touch. Transfer to a wire rack to cool completely.

To make the frosting, put the butter in a bowl and beat together until light and fluffy. Sift in the confectioners' sugar and beat together until well mixed, gradually beating in the milk.

When the cupcakes are cold, place the frosting in a pastry bag fitted with a large star tip. Pipe the frosting on top of each cupcake, then add a cherry to decorate.

Pistachio Cupcakes with Tangy Lime Frosting

makes 16

generous ¾ cup unsalted pistachio nuts

½ cup butter, softened

¾ cup superfine sugar

1 cup self-rising flour

2 eggs, lightly beaten

4 tbsp Greek yogurt

1 tbsp pistachio nuts, chopped, to decorate

frosting

½ cup butter, softened

2 tbsp sweetened lime juice

few drops green food coloring (optional)

1¾ cups confectioners' sugar

Preheat the oven to 350°F/180°C. Line two 12-hole muffin pans with 16 paper liners or put 16 double-layer paper liners on a baking sheet.

Put the pistachio nuts in a food processor or blender and process for a few seconds until finely ground. Add the butter, sugar, flour, eggs, and yogurt and process until evenly mixed. Spoon the batter into the paper liners.

Bake the cupcakes in the preheated oven for 20–25 minutes, or until well risen and springy to the touch. Transfer to a wire rack and let cool completely.

To make the frosting, put the butter, lime juice, and food coloring (if using) in a bowl and beat until light and fluffy. Sift in the confectioners' sugar and beat until smooth. Swirl the frosting over each cupcake and sprinkle with the chopped pistachio nuts to decorate.

Banana & Pecan Cupcakes

makes 24

1⅔ cups all-purpose flour

1¼ tsp baking powder

¼ tsp baking soda

2 ripe bananas

½ cup butter, softened,
or soft margarine

generous ½ cup superfine
sugar

½ tsp vanilla extract

2 eggs, lightly beaten

¼ cup sour cream

generous ⅓ cup pecans,
coarsely chopped

1 tbsp pecans, finely chopped,
to decorate

frosting

½ cup butter, softened

1 cup confectioners' sugar

Preheat the oven to 375°F/190°C. Line two 12-hole muffin pans with 24 paper liners or put 12 double-layer paper liners on a baking sheet.

Sift together the flour, baking powder, and baking soda. Place the bananas in a separate bowl and mash with a fork.

Place the butter, sugar, and vanilla extract in a large bowl and beat together until light and fluffy, then gradually beat in the eggs. Stir in the mashed bananas and sour cream. Fold in the flour mixture and chopped nuts. Spoon the batter into the paper liners.

Bake in the preheated oven for 20 minutes, or until well risen and springy to the touch. Transfer to a wire rack to cool completely.

To make the frosting, place the butter in a bowl and beat until light and fluffy. Sift in the confectioners' sugar and mix together well. Spread the frosting on top of each cupcake and sprinkle with the pecans before serving.

Carrot & Orange Cupcakes

makes 12

½ cup butter, softened,
or soft margarine

generous ½ cup light brown
sugar

juice and finely grated rind
of 1 small orange

2 large eggs, lightly beaten

generous 1 cup grated carrot

¼ cup walnut pieces,
coarsely chopped

1 cup all-purpose flour

1 tsp ground pumpkin
pie spice

1½ tsp baking powder

frosting

1¼ cups mascarpone cheese

¼ cup confectioners' sugar

grated rind of 1 large orange

Preheat the oven to 350°F/180°C. Line a 12-hole muffin pan with 12 paper liners or put 12 double-layer paper liners on a baking sheet.

Place the butter, sugar, and orange rind in a bowl and beat together until light and fluffy, then gradually beat in the eggs. Squeeze any excess liquid from the carrots and add to the mixture with the walnuts and orange juice. Stir until well mixed. Sift in the flour, pumpkin pie spice, and baking powder and fold in. Spoon the batter into the paper liners.

Bake in the preheated oven for 25 minutes, or until well risen and springy to the touch. Transfer to a wire rack to cool completely.

To make the frosting, place the mascarpone cheese, confectioners' sugar, and orange rind in a large bowl and beat together until they are well mixed.

When the cupcakes are cold, spread the frosting on top of each cupcake, swirling it with a round-bladed knife.

Festive Fancies

Birthday Party Cupcakes

makes 24

1 cup butter, softened,
or soft margarine

generous 1 cup superfine
sugar

4 eggs

1⅔ cups self-rising flour

a variety of candies and
chocolates, sugar-coated
chocolates, dried fruits, edible
sugar flower shapes, cake
decorating sprinkles, silver or
gold dragées

various tubes of colored
decorating icing

candles and candleholders
(optional), to decorate

frosting
¾ cup butter, softened
3 cups confectioners' sugar

Preheat the oven to 350°F/180°C. Line two 12-hole muffin pans with 24 paper liners or put 24 double-layer paper liners on a baking sheet.

Place the butter, sugar, eggs, and flour in a large bowl and beat together until just smooth. Spoon the batter into the paper liners.

Bake in the preheated oven for 15–20 minutes, or until well risen and springy to the touch.

To make the frosting, place the butter in a bowl and beat until light and fluffy. Sift in the confectioners' sugar and beat together until smooth. When the cupcakes are cold, spread the frosting on top of each cupcake, then decorate as you like and place a candle in the top of each, if using.

Valentine Heart Cupcakes

makes 6

6 tbsp butter, softened,
or soft margarine

½ cup superfine sugar

½ tsp vanilla extract

2 eggs, lightly beaten

½ cup all-purpose flour

1 tbsp unsweetened cocoa

1 tsp baking powder

6 chocolate flower
decorations

marzipan hearts

confectioners' sugar,
for dusting

1¼ oz/35 g marzipan

red food coloring (liquid or
paste)

frosting

4 tbsp butter, softened

1 cup confectioners' sugar

1 oz/25 g semisweet
chocolate, melted

To make the marzipan hearts, line a baking sheet with parchment paper and lightly dust with confectioners' sugar. Knead the marzipan until pliable, then add a few drops of red coloring and knead until evenly colored. Roll out the marzipan to a thickness of ¼ inch/5 mm on a surface dusted with confectioners' sugar. Cut out 6 hearts with a small heart-shaped cutter and place on the sheet. Let stand for 3–4 hours.

To make the cupcakes, preheat the oven to 350°F/180°C. Line a 12-hole muffin pan with 6 paper liners or put 6 double-layer paper liners on a baking sheet.

Place the butter, sugar, and vanilla extract in a large bowl and beat together until light and fluffy, then gradually beat in the eggs. Sift in the flour, cocoa, and baking powder and fold into the batter. Spoon the batter into the paper liners.

Bake in the preheated oven for 20–25 minutes, or until well risen and firm to the touch. Transfer to a wire rack to cool completely.

To make the frosting, place the butter in a bowl and beat until light and fluffy. Sift in the confectioners' sugar and beat until smooth. Add the melted chocolate and beat until well mixed. Spread the frosting on top of each cupcake and decorate with a chocolate flower and a marzipan heart.

Easter Cupcakes

makes 12

½ cup butter, softened, or soft margarine

generous ½ cup superfine sugar

2 eggs, lightly beaten

⅔ cup self-rising flour

¼ cup unsweetened cocoa

9 oz/260 g mini sugar-coated chocolate eggs, to decorate

frosting

6 tbsp butter, softened

1 cup confectioners' sugar

1 tbsp milk

2–3 drops vanilla extract

Preheat the oven to 350°F/180°C. Line a 12-hole muffin pan with 12 paper liners or put 12 double-layer paper liners on a baking sheet.

Place the butter and sugar in a large bowl and beat together until light and fluffy, then gradually beat in the eggs. Sift in the flour and cocoa and fold into the batter. Spoon the batter into the paper liners.

Bake in the preheated oven for 15–20 minutes, or until well risen and springy to the touch. Transfer to a wire rack to cool completely.

To make the frosting, place the butter in a bowl and beat together until light and fluffy. Sift in the confectioners' sugar and beat together until well mixed, adding the milk and vanilla extract.

When the cupcakes are cold, place the frosting in a pastry bag fitted with a large star tip, and pipe a circle around the edge of each cupcake to form a nest. Place chocolate eggs in the center of each nest to decorate.

Baby Shower Cupcakes with Sugared Almonds

makes 24

1¾ cups butter, softened

2 cups superfine sugar

finely grated rind of 2 lemons

8 eggs, lightly beaten

3 cups self-rising flour

24 sugared almonds,
to decorate

icing

3 cups confectioners' sugar

6–8 tsp hot water

red or blue food coloring
(liquid or paste)

Preheat the oven to 350°F/180°C. Line two 12-hole muffin pans with 24 paper liners or put 24 double-layer paper liners on a baking sheet.

Place the butter, sugar, and lemon rind in a large bowl and beat together until light and fluffy, then gradually beat in the eggs. Sift in the flour and fold into the mixture. Spoon the batter into the paper liners.

Bake in the preheated oven for 20–25 minutes, or until well risen and springy to the touch.

When the cupcakes are cold, make the icing. Sift the confectoners' sugar into a bowl, add the hot water, and stir until smooth and thick enough to coat the back of a wooden spoon. Dip a skewer into the red or blue food coloring and stir it into the icing until it is evenly colored pink or pale blue. Spoon the icing on top of each cupcake. Top each with a sugared almond to decorate and let set for about 30 minutes.

Springtime Cupcakes

makes 24

½ cup plus 2 tbsp butter,
softened,
or soft margarine

¾ cup superfine sugar

1 tsp vanilla extract

2 large eggs, lightly beaten

1 cup self-rising flour

generous ¼ cup cornstarch

topping

4 oz/115 g white ready-to-
use rolled fondant

yellow and green food
colorings (liquid or paste)

2⅔ cups confectioners' sugar

about 3 tbsp cold water

colored sprinkles

Preheat the oven to 375°F/190°C. Line two 12-hole muffin pans with 24 paper liners or put 24 double-layer paper liners on a baking sheet.

Place the butter and sugar in a large bowl and beat together until light and fluffy, then beat in the vanilla extract. Gradually beat in the eggs. Sift in the flour and cornstarch and fold into the batter. Spoon the batter into the paper liners.

Bake in the preheated oven for 12–15 minutes, or until well risen and springy to the touch. Transfer to a wire rack to cool completely.

To make the topping, divide the fondant in half and color one half pale yellow. Roll out both halves, then use the sides of a round cookie cutter to cut out white and yellow petal shapes. Set aside.

Sift the confectioners' sugar into a bowl and mix with the water until smooth. Place half of the icing in a small pastry bag fitted with a small, plain tip. Divide the remaining icing in half and color one portion yellow and the other green.

Cover 12 cupcakes with yellow icing and 12 with green icing. Arrange white petals on top of the yellow icing to form flowers. Pipe a little blob of white icing into the center of each flower, then add a few colored sprinkles on top of the white icing to form the center of the flower. Arrange the yellow petals on the green icing and decorate in the same way. Let set.

Halloween Cupcakes

makes 12

½ cup butter, softened,
or soft margarine

generous ½ cup superfine
sugar

2 eggs

generous ¾ cup self-rising
flour

indoor sparklers, to decorate
(optional)

topping

7 oz/200 g orange ready-to-
use rolled fondant

confectioners' sugar,
for dusting

2 oz/55 g black ready-to-use
rolled fondant

tube of black decorating icing

tube of white decorating icing

Preheat the oven to 350°F/180°C. Line a 12-hole muffin pan with 12 paper liners or put 12 double-layer paper liners on a baking sheet.

Place the butter, sugar, eggs, and flour in a large bowl and beat together until smooth. Spoon the batter into the paper liners.

Bake in the preheated oven for 15–20 minutes, or until well risen and springy to the touch. Transfer to a wire rack to cool completely.

When the cupcakes are cold, knead the orange fondant until pliable, then roll out on a surface dusted with confectioners' sugar.

Cut out 12 rounds with a 2¼-inch/5.5-cm round cutter, rerolling the fondant as necessary. Place a round on top of each cupcake.

Roll out the black fondant on a surface dusted with confectioners' sugar. Cut out 12 rounds with a 1¼-inch/3-cm round cutter and place them in the center of the cakes. Using black decorating icing, pipe 8 legs onto each spider, and draw eyes and a mouth with white decorating icing.

Christmas Cupcakes

makes 12

generous ½ cup butter,
softened

1 cup superfine sugar

4–6 drops almond extract

4 eggs, lightly beaten

1 generous cup self-rising
flour

½ cup ground almonds

topping

1 lb/450 g white ready-to-use
rolled fondant

2 oz/55 g green ready-to-use
rolled fondant

1 oz/25 g red ready-to-use
rolled fondant

confectioners' sugar,
for dusting

Preheat the oven to 350°F/180°C. Line a 12-hole muffin pan with 12 paper liners or put 12 double-layer paper liners on a baking sheet.

Place the butter, sugar, and almond extract in a large bowl and beat together until light and fluffy, then gradually beat in the eggs. Sift in the flour and fold into the mixture, then fold in the ground almonds. Spoon the batter into the paper liners.

Bake in the preheated oven for 20 minutes, or until well risen and springy to the touch. Transfer to a wire rack to cool completely.

When the cupcakes are cold, knead the white fondant until pliable, then roll out on a surface lightly dusted with confectioners' sugar. Cut out 12 rounds with a 2¾-inch/7-cm plain round cutter, rerolling the fondant as necessary. Place a round on top of each cupcake.

Roll out the green fondant on a surface lightly dusted with confectioners' sugar. Cut out 24 leaves with a holly leaf-shaped cutter, rerolling the fondant as necessary. Brush each leaf with a little cooled boiled water and place 2 leaves on top of each cupcake. Roll the red fondant between the palms of your hands to form 36 berries and place 3 in the center of the leaves on each cupcake to decorate.

Festive Cupcakes

makes 14

½ cup mixed dried fruit

1 tsp finely grated orange rind

2 tbsp brandy or orange juice

6 tbsp butter, softened

scant ½ cup brown sugar

1 large egg, lightly beaten

generous ¾ cup self-rising flour

1 tsp ground allspice

1 tbsp silver dragées, to decorate

icing

¾ cup confectioners' sugar

2 tbsp orange juice

Put the mixed dried fruit, orange rind, and brandy in a small bowl, cover, and let soak for 1 hour.

Preheat the oven to 375°F/190°C. Line two 12-hole muffin pans with 14 paper liners or put 14 double-layer paper liners on a baking sheet.

Put the butter and sugar in a bowl and beat together until light and fluffy. Gradually beat in the egg. Sift in the flour and allspice and, using a metal spoon, fold them into the batter followed by the soaked fruit. Spoon the batter into the paper liners.

Bake the cupcakes in the preheated oven for 15–20 minutes, or until well risen and springy to the touch. Transfer to a wire rack to cool completely.

To make the icing, sift the confectioners' sugar into a bowl and gradually mix in enough orange juice until the mixture is smooth and thick enough to coat the back of a wooden spoon. Using a teaspoon, drizzle the icing in a zigzag pattern over the cupcakes. Decorate with the silver dragées. Let set.

Wedding Day Fancy Favors

makes 12

scant ½ cup soft butter

½ cup superfine sugar

2 eggs, lightly beaten

scant 1 cup self-rising flour, sifted

½ tsp vanilla extract

1–2 tbsp milk

topping

confectioners' sugar, for dusting

8 oz/225 g white ready-to-use rolled fondant

3 tbsp honey, warmed

2–3 drops pink food coloring (liquid or paste)

tube of green writing icing

Turn on the oven to 400°F/ 200°C. Put 12 paper liners into a 12-cup muffin pan or put 12 double-layer paper liners on a baking sheet.

Put the butter and superfine sugar into a bowl and beat together for 1–2 minutes, until pale and creamy. Gradually add the eggs and continue beating. Fold in the flour using a metal spoon. Stir in the vanilla extract and milk.

Put a spoonful of the batter into each liner. Bake in the preheated oven for 15-20 minutes, or until well risen and springy to the touch. Remove them from the oven and let them cool for 5 minutes in the pan, then move them to a wire rack to cool completely.

Dust the counter with some confectioners' sugar. Roll out all but one-eighth of the fondant to 11 x 8 inches/28 x 20 cm. Use a cookie cutter to stamp out 12 rounds. Brush the cake tops with some honey and stick on the rounds.

For the rosebuds, knead the remaining fondant with the food coloring. Roll out strips of fondant to 2½ x ½ inch/6 x 1 cm. Roll up from one end and stick onto the cake with a dab of honey. Draw on a stalk and leaves with the writing icing.

Gold & Silver Anniversary Cupcakes

makes 24

1 cup butter, softened
generous 1 cup superfine sugar
1 tsp vanilla extract
4 large eggs, lightly beaten
1⅔ cups self-rising flour
5 tbsp milk
silver or gold dragées, to decorate

frosting
¾ cup butter
3 cups confectioners' sugar

Preheat the oven to 350°F/180°C. Line two 12-hole muffin pans with 24 silver or gold foil cake liners or put 24 double-layer foil liners on a baking sheet.

Place the butter, sugar, and vanilla extract in a large bowl and beat together until light and fluffy, then gradually beat in the eggs. Sift in the flour and fold into the mixture with the milk. Spoon the batter into the foil liners.

Bake in the preheated oven for 15–20 minutes, or until well risen and springy to the touch. Transfer to a wire rack to cool completely.

To make the frosting, place the butter in a large bowl and beat together until light and fluffy. Sift in the confectioners' sugar and beat together until well mixed. Place the topping in a pastry bag fitted with a medium star-shaped tip.

When the cupcakes are cold, pipe circles of frosting on top of each cupcake to cover the tops and sprinkle over the silver or gold dragées, to decorate.